PHILO T. FARNSWORTH

by Ellen Labrecque

PEBBLE

a capstone imprint

Pebble Explore is published by Pebble, an imprint of Capstone.
1710 Roe Crest Drive
North Mankato, Minnesota 56003
www.capstonepub.com

**Library of Congress Cataloging-in-Publication Data is available on the
Library of Congress website.**
ISBN 978-1-9771-3209-3 (library binding)
ISBN 978-1-9771-5473-6 (ebook pdf)

Summary: Describes the life of inventor of the television, Philo T. Farnsworth,
including his early life, challenges, and major accomplishments.

Image Credits
Alamy: Matthew Kiernan, 19, The Reading Room, 11; Associated Press: The
Journal Gazette/Matt Sullivan, 27; Getty Images: Bettmann, 17, 20, 22, 23,
Corbis/George Rinhart, 21, Popular Science, 9, The LIFE Picture Collection, 5,
Underwood Archive, cover, 1, 25; iStockphoto: Aaron Hawkins, 16; Library
of Congress: 7, 13; Shutterstock: catwalker, 26, Donna Milner, 6, Gino Santa
Maria, 15, kapooklook01 (geometric background), cover, back cover, 2, 29,
Mykola Mazuryk, 14; Wikipedia: Library of Congress, 29

Editorial Credits
Editor: Erika L. Shores; Designer: Elyse White; Media Researcher: Svetlana
Zhurkin; Production Specialist: Spencer Rosio

Printed and bound in China. 4205

Table of Contents

Words in **bold** are in the glossary.

Who Was Philo T. Farnsworth?

Philo T. Farnsworth was a smart **inventor**. He came up with ideas to build new machines. He is most famous for inventing the television.

Philo thought of the idea when he was a teenager. But for a long time, nobody even knew who Philo was. A company named Radio Corporation of America (RCA) said their workers came up with the idea for television. It was only after Philo's death that people learned he was the inventor.

Childhood

Philo was born in Indian Creek, Utah, on August 19, 1906. His father, Lewis Edwin Farnsworth, and his mother, Serena Amanda Bastian, lived in a log cabin. It had no **electricity**. The house didn't have light or heat. Philo was the oldest of five children. His family were farmers.

A log house in Utah

People boarding a train around the year 1900

Young Philo loved to learn new things. At age 3, Philo went with his dad to see a train. When Philo came home, he drew pictures of both the inside and outside of the train. He wanted to understand how the train worked.

By the time Philo was six, he knew he wanted to invent machines. In spring 1919, Philo and his family moved to a farm near Rigby, Idaho. The new house had electricity. Philo couldn't wait to learn about it.

Philo found stacks of old science magazines in the attic of the house. Stories in the magazines explained how things worked.

American magazine Popular Science was first published in 1872.

Philo taught himself many things by reading. He also learned from watching adults. One day when Philo was 12, the farm's **generator** stopped working. The generator is what gave the farm its electrical power. Philo had watched a worker fix it once already. Philo knew he could fix the generator.

Philo saw the parts weren't broken. They just had too much grease on them. Philo wiped the grease off each part. He then put the generator back together. It worked again!

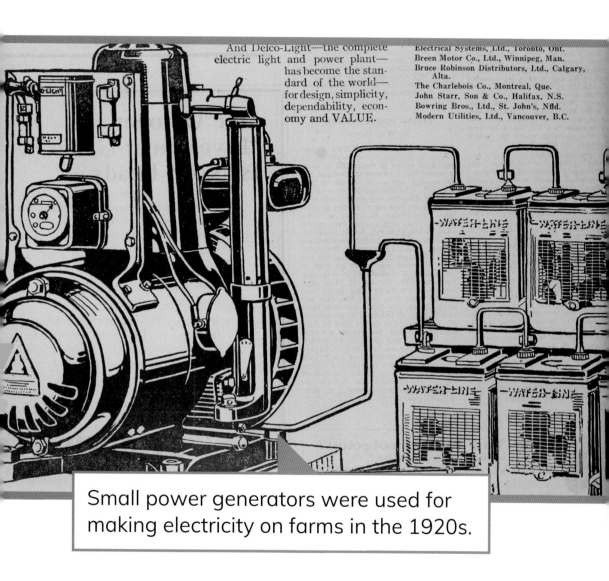

And Delco-Light—the complete electric light and power plant—has become the standard of the world—for design, simplicity, dependability, economy and VALUE.

Electrical Systems, Ltd., Toronto, Ont.
Breen Motor Co., Ltd., Winnipeg, Man.
Bruce Robinson Distributors, Ltd., Calgary, Alta.
The Charlebois Co., Montreal, Que.
John Starr, Son & Co., Halifax, N.S.
Bowring Bros., Ltd., St. John's, Nfld.
Modern Utilities, Ltd., Vancouver, B.C.

Small power generators were used for making electricity on farms in the 1920s.

A Clever Idea

During the 1920s, people listened to the radio. They listened to hear the news. They listened to hear music and stories. It was a fun way for families to spend time together.

Radio works by turning sound into **air waves**, or electrical signals. A radio station sends waves through the air. A radio on the other end picks up the waves and turns them into sound. Many inventors believed images could be sent the same way. They just didn't know how yet.

A young boy listening to the radio in 1922

Big Ideas

One day when Philo was 14, he was plowing a potato field on the family farm. As he plowed, he made line after line in the soil. Philo looked back at these lines.

A plowed farm field

An idea sprang up in Philo's head. He thought he could break images down line by line too. He could grab these lines of light as **electrons**. The lines could be sent through the air waves. Then they could be put back together as pictures to appear on screens. This is how television could work, Philo thought.

Philo thought of sending electronic signals to a screen as lines.

In 1923, when Philo was 18, his family moved back to Utah. Just a year later, Philo's dad died.

After finishing high school, Philo went to Brigham Young University in Provo, Utah. During this time, Philo met Elma "Pem" Gardner. They fell in love. Philo and Pem married on May 27, 1926. Philo did not finish at Brigham Young. He left early to help his family.

One of the buildings at Brigham Young University

Pem and Philo in 1934

To make money, Philo repaired radios. But in his extra time, he worked on making his television dream come true. Philo and Pem worked together. Pem helped Philo make drawings of his ideas and plans.

The Real Inventor

Philo thought television would help bring people together. They would watch the same shows and hear the same stories. They would begin to feel more alike than different. He thought television could help bring about world peace.

Philo told people about his television idea. Some of the people gave Philo money to help him build the first one. With this money, Philo also hired workers to help him.

Philo worked in his lab in San Francisco, California.

Philo and his team worked day and night. On September 7, 1927, they finally did it. They sent the first electronic television image. The image could then be seen on a screen. It was only a single line, but now everybody saw that it was possible. Philo was just 21 years old.

Philo with his television in 1928

A woman watching an early TV made by RCA in 1928

RCA workers were trying to invent television at the same time as Philo. RCA was one of the biggest companies in the United States. It had a lot of money. The people at RCA said they were the first to invent television, not Philo.

Philo and RCA got into a fight. They went to court. Each told their side of the story in front of a judge. In 1935, Philo was declared the real inventor. Unfortunately, Philo didn't have enough money to make and sell a lot of TVs. RCA had plenty. They did what Philo wanted to do. RCA made even more money from Philo's invention.

Philo showed how his television worked in 1930.

Philo in his office in 1940

Philo was upset. But he tried to move forward with his life. He started his own company. He tried to make and sell as many televisions as RCA. He was never able to do so.

Philo's company went **bankrupt** in 1949. This meant Philo ran out of money and had to close his business.

Philo kept thinking up other ideas. He made an electron **microscope** and an infant **incubator**. The incubator helped keep babies safe when they were born too early.

Throughout the rest of his life, Philo tried to start other companies. But he wasn't good at business. He was simply good at the inventing part. On March 11, 1971, Philo died. He was 64 years old.

Philo in 1950

Remembering Philo

After Philo died, Pem worked to make sure people remembered her husband. Pem told her husband's story to newspaper and TV reporters. She was his biggest fan. It worked. Thanks to Pem, Philo is now remembered as the man who brought television into people's homes.

Philo was on a U.S. postal stamp in 1983.

Pem with Philo's statue, photo, and journal in 1999

Important Dates

August 19, 1906	Philo T. Farnsworth is born in Indian Creek, Utah.
1919	Philo and his family move to Rigby, Idaho.
1921	Philo comes up with the idea for television while plowing potato fields.
1926	Philo marries Pem Gardner on May 27.
1927	Philo sends the first television image on September 7.
1935	Philo beats RCA and wins the right to continue to make televisions.
1949	Philo's company shuts down because it doesn't have enough money to continue.
March 11, 1971	Philo dies at age 64.

Fast Facts

Name:
Philo T. Farnsworth

Role:
inventor

Life dates:
August 19, 1906 to March 11, 1971

Key accomplishments:
Philo invented television. He also invented other things, such as an electron microscope and an infant incubator.

Glossary

air waves (AIR WEYVZ)—the way radio and television is made to work

bankrupt (BANGK-ruhpt)—when a company or person runs out of money

electricity (ih-lek-TRIS-ih-tee)—the energy you get when electrons flow from place to place

electron (ih-LEK-tron)—a very small particle that carries a charge of electricity

generator (JEN-uh-rey-ter)—a machine that converts one form of energy into another, creating electricity

incubator (IN-kyuh-bey-ter)—an enclosed case that keeps babies safe inside

inventor (in-VENT-er)—a person who invents or creates new things

microscope (MAHY-kruh-skohp)—an instrument that magnifies objects that would be too small to see with the naked eye

Read More

Kenney, Karen Latchana. *Who Invented Television?: Sarnoff vs. Farnsworth*. Minneapolis: Lerner Publishing, 2018.

London, Martha. *Philo Farnsworth*. Minneapolis: Pop!, a division of ABDO, 2020.

Internet Sites

Inventors Hall of Fame
invent.org

Philo Farnsworth's Story
kidzworld.com/article/19948-the-story-of-philo-farnsworth-the-kid-who-invented-tv

Index